Understanding Autism: A Simple And Friendly Guide

Here is to celebrating every mind and every journey. May this book bring understanding, hope and a reminder that every perspective matters.

A. Suleman
— x —

Aisha Idris Suleman

Understanding Autism: A Simple And Friendly Guide © 2025 Aisha Idris Suleman

All rights reserved.

No part of this publication may be reproduced, stored in a retrieval system, or transmitted, in any form or by any means, electronic, mechanical, photocopying, recording or otherwise, without the prior written permission of the author.

Aisha Idris Suleman asserts the moral right to be identified as author of this work.

To my son – you are my greatest teacher, my inspiration and the reason why this book exists. Your light shines brighter than words can express. To every individual on the autism spectrum – may your voices be heard, your differences be embraced and your brilliance be recognised. To the families, friends and caregivers walking on this path – may you find strength, patience and joy in the journey. Finally, to all those who seek to understand – may this guide open hearts, build bridges and spark compassion.

Contents

ACKNOWLEDGEMENT 6

PREFACE 7

Introduction 8

Chapter 1: What Is Autism? 9

Chapter 2: Early Signs And Diagnosis 11

Chapter 3: How People With Autism Experience The World 14

Chapter 4: Everyday Support Strategies 18

Chapter 5: Education And Learning 23

Chapter 6: Autism In Teenagers And Adults 28

Chapter 7: Talking About Autism 33

Chapter 8: Myths And Truths About Autism 37

Chapter 9: How To Be A Good Ally 41

Chapter 10: Resources And Next Steps 45

ACKNOWLEDGEMENT

Writing this book has been a deeply personal journey and I am profoundly grateful to the many people who supported me along the way.

First and foremost, to my beloved son – thank you for being exactly who you are. Your courage, honesty and unique view of the world continues to teach me more than any textbook. This book is for you and because of you.

To my family, friends and fans – thank you for your unwavering love and encouragement. Your support gave me the strength to keep writing, even when it can be difficult at times.

To the autism community – thank you for your openness, your advocacy and your willingness to share your experiences. Your voices are essential and I am honoured to help amplify them in whatever way I can.

To the schools, teachers, educators, therapists and specialists who work every day to support neurodivergent individuals – your dedication inspires hope and makes a difference in countless lives.

PREFACE

Autism is not a mystery. It is not a tragedy and it is definitely not something that needs to be 'fixed.'

It is simply a different way of thinking, feeling and experiencing the world.

I wrote this book because my beautiful and smart son is autistic. When he was first diagnosed, I felt like there was so much information out there, yet so little of it was simple, kind or easy to understand. Some of it was cold and clinical. Some of it focused only on problems. A lot of it forgot that autistic people are people first; full of life, love, challenges, strengths and beauty.

This book is the resource I wish I had right from the beginning.

It is a gentle and honest guide for anyone who wants to understand autism better. Whether you are a parent, teacher, friend or just someone who cares, it is written with you in mind. No complicated language and no fear. Just real talk, clear explanations and practical ways to be more supportive, inclusive and kind.

Most of all, it is written with deep love and respect for my son, as well as for every autistic person who deserves to be seen, accepted and celebrated just as they are.

Autism is not something to fear. It is something to understand.

LET'S BEGIN!

Introduction

Autism can be a confusing word when you first hear it. For some, it is a diagnosis they or their child received. For others, it is something they have heard about, but don't fully understand it. This book is here to help without overwhelming you.

You don't need to be a doctor or a specialist to understand autism. You just need a little guidance, a little patience and a willingness to learn. Whether you are a parent like myself, a teacher, a friend or someone who just wants to understand more, this guide is for you.

Autism is a spectrum, which means it looks different in every person. Some people with autism speak a lot, whilst others don't speak at all. Some love routine, whilst others are flexible. Some need help every day, whilst others live independently. Whatever the case, all of these people deserve to be understood, respected and supported.

Let's get started!

Chapter 1: What Is Autism?

Autism or Autism Spectrum Disorder (ASD) is a way of describing how some people think, feel and experience the world. It is not an illness or a disease, which needs to be clarified! It is a difference in how the brain works.

People with autism might:

- See details that others miss
- Prefer routines and familiar patterns
- Find it hard to understand social cues (like facial expressions or tone of voice)
- Have strong interests or hobbies
- React differently to sounds, lights or textures

Remember, not every autistic person is the same. Autism is a spectrum, which means it includes a wide range of experiences, needs and strengths.

AUTISM IS NOT:

- Caused by bad parenting
- Something you can catch
- Something that can be cured

Autism is a lifelong condition, but with support and understanding, people with autism can thrive at home, in school, at work and in the community.

What Causes Autism?

Doctors and scientists are not exactly sure what causes autism, but they know it is not one single thing. It involves a mix of genetics and brain development. What is important to know is that no one is to blame.

Myths vs Facts:

- **Myth:** All autistic people are the same.
  Fact: Autism is different for everyone. That is why it is called a spectrum.

- **Myth:** People with autism don't feel emotions.
  Fact: They do, but they might express them differently.

- **Myth:** People with autism can't succeed in life.
  Fact: Many people with autism are artists, engineers, writers, parents, teachers and more!

Chapter 2: Early Signs And Diagnosis

One of the most common questions people ask is: 'How do I know if a child might be autistic?' The truth is, autism can show up in many different ways. Some signs may appear in infancy, while others become more noticeable when a child starts school or interacts more with others.

Understanding the early signs can help families and caregivers get the right support sooner, which can make a big difference.

Early Signs In Young Children

Every child develops at their own pace, but here are some signs that might show up in babies or toddlers:

- **Not responding to their name** by 12 months
- **Avoiding eye contact** or not smiling back when smiled at
- **Delayed speech** or not using gestures like pointing or waving
- **Repeating actions** over and over, such as flapping hands or spinning objects
- **Strong reactions** to certain sounds, textures or lights
- **Lining up toys** instead of playing with them in a typical way
- **Preferring to play alone** rather than with other children

Noticing one of these signs does not necessarily mean a child is autistic for sure, but noticing several of these signs might be a good reason to talk to a doctor.

What Happens During A Diagnosis?

If you or someone you care for shows signs of autism, a healthcare professional, usually a paediatrician, psychologist or specialist, can do an evaluation. Here is what that process might include:

- **Interviews and checklists** about the person's behaviour and development
- **Observing how they interact**, play and communicate
- **Developmental tests** to check learning, language and movement skills

A diagnosis is not about labelling someone. It is about understanding how they see the world, so they can get the right kind of support.

Why Early Diagnosis Matters

Getting diagnosed early does not change who a child is, but it can open the door to helpful resources like:

- **Speech Therapy**
- **Occupational Therapy**

- **Social Skills Support**

- **Education Planning**

Early support can help children grow into confident and capable individuals. The sooner we understand their needs, the better we can help them thrive.

For Older Kids And Adults

Sometimes, autism is not noticed until later on in life, especially in people who have learned to hide their struggles. This is common in girls, teens or adults who have always felt different, but never knew why.

Getting a diagnosis at any age can bring clarity, self-understanding and a sense of relief. It can help people find the right communities and strategies.

A Word Of Encouragement

If you are worried about your child or someone you know then remember, wondering is not the same as knowing. It is okay to ask questions and seek help. It is always better to know because knowledge brings options, understanding and peace of mind.

Chapter 3: How People With Autism Experience The World

People with autism often experience the world in a different, but equally valid way. They might notice things others do not, or they might feel overwhelmed in situations that seem normal to most people. Understanding these differences helps us to be more supportive and compassionate.

This chapter will give you a better picture of what life might feel like for someone on the autism spectrum.

1. Sensory Differences

Imagine if everyday things, such as bright lights, loud noises or scratchy clothing felt extra strong to you. That is what sensory sensitivity can be like for many autistic people.

They might:

- Cover their ears if they hear loud sounds, such as hand dryers or sirens
- Avoid certain textures in food or clothes
- Be bothered by flickering lights, strong smells or crowded places
- Seek out certain sensations, such as spinning, squeezing or touching soft things

Some people are **hypersensitive** (too sensitive), whereas others are **hyposensitive** (not sensitive enough and may seek more stimulation).

Tip: If someone avoids certain environments or reacts strongly to something, it is not rudeness, it might be sensory overload.

2. Social Communication Differences

Social rules, such as making eye contact, taking turns in conversations or understanding sarcasm can be confusing or even exhausting for autistic people.

They might:

- Prefer direct and literal language
- Take longer to process what someone says
- Not always show facial expressions or body language in the expected way
- Avoid eye contact, not because they are being rude, but because they just find it uncomfortable

Here is the truth though, autistic people often care deeply about others. They may just express it differently, compared to those that are not on the spectrum.

3. Routines And Predictability

Many autistic individuals feel more comfortable when life is predictable. They may have strong routines and get anxious when those routines are disrupted.

This can look like:

- Wanting to eat the same food every day
- Following the same bedtime routine every night
- Getting upset if plans change suddenly
- Using the same route to go to school everyday

Routines give a sense of safety and control in a world that can sometimes feel overwhelming.

4. Special Interests And Deep Focus

Many people with autism have strong interests in certain topics and they often know a lot about them!

These can be:

- Trains, animals, space, maps or numbers
- TV shows, video games or books
- Art, music or machines

These interests are not just hobbies. They can be a source of joy, comfort and even future careers. Supporting someone's passion can help build their confidence and connection with others.

5. Emotional Expression

Autistic people experience a full range of emotions, such as joy, sadness, frustration or love, but they might show them in ways, which others don't expect.

For example:

- They might not smile when happy, but flap their hands or bounce

- They may cry or have a meltdown when overwhelmed, not to gain attention, but because it has become too much for them

- They might not say 'I love you,' but show it through actions, such as sharing their favourite toy or fact

Reminder: Just because emotions look different, it does not mean they are not there!

Different, Not Less

Autism is not a problem to be fixed; it is a way of being. When we take time to understand how autistic people see the world, we create more accepting, flexible and supportive environments.

The goal is not to change autistic people, it is to understand and respect them.

Chapter 4: Everyday Support Strategies

Supporting someone with autism does not have to be complicated. In fact, small actions can make a big difference. Whether you are a parent, teacher, sibling, friend or caregiver, the goal is to build trust, reduce stress and create a safe and respectful environment.

This chapter will give you simple and practical strategies to help autistic people feel understood and supported.

1. Create Predictable Routines

Many autistic people feel more comfortable when they know what to expect.

Try:

- Using **visual timetables** (such as, pictures or charts showing daily activities)
- Giving **advance notice** before changes (such as saying, 'In 10 minutes, it will be time to leave the park')
- Sticking to regular routines for meals, bedtime or transitions

Even small routines can create a strong sense of safety.

2. Communicate Clearly And Calmly

Autistic people often understand best when communication is simple, clear and honest.

Do:

- Use **clear and direct language** (such as, 'Please hang up your coat' instead of 'Why don't you put that where it goes?')
- Be **patient** and give them time to respond
- Use **visual aids** or gestures when needed

Avoid:

- Using sarcasm or vague language (such as, 'Pull your socks up' to mean 'try harder')
- Speaking too fast or giving too many instructions at once

Everyone processes communication differently. Slowing down and simplifying can go a long way.

3. Support Sensory Needs

Respecting someone's sensory preferences can make their day easier and more peaceful.

You can:

- Offer **noise-cancelling headphones** if loud places are stressful
- Let them wear clothes that feel comfortable to them
- Create **quiet spaces** to calm down when things get overwhelming

- Allow fidget toys or movement breaks if it helps them stay focused

Ask what works best for them and always listen to their answers.

4. Don't Force Social Interaction

It is okay if someone with autism prefers alone time or does not socialise like others do. You can still help them build social skills in gentle and respectful ways.

Try:

- Encouraging shared activities around their **special interests**
- Practicing **turn-taking** or **conversation skills** through games and stories
- Accepting non-traditional ways of connecting (such as, parallel play or sharing facts instead of asking questions)

Let them lead the way. Social success is different for everyone.

5. Focus On Strengths

Everyone is good at something, even if it is not obvious straight away. Noticing and encouraging someone's strengths can boost their confidence.

Celebrate:

- Creativity, memory, honesty and attention to detail

- A deep interest in a topic
- Progress, no matter how small

Instead of focusing only on what is hard, recognise and nurture what is great.

6. Stay Calm During Meltdowns

A meltdown is not a tantrum. It is not about gaining attention, but a reaction to too much stress, noise, change or emotion.

In those moments:

- Stay calm and do not yell or punish
- Offer quiet support and remove triggers if possible
- Let them recover at their own pace

When things have calmed down, you can talk about what happened and how to help next time.

7. Be Kind To Yourself Too

Supporting someone with autism can be deeply rewarding, but it can also be challenging. That is okay.

Remember:

- You will not always get it right and that is normal
- It is okay to ask for help from therapists, teachers or support groups

- Take breaks and care for your own mental health too

The more supported you feel, the better support you can give.

Final Thought

At the heart of all these strategies is one simple idea, **respect**. Respect the person's feelings, their needs, their strengths and their differences.

Chapter 5: Education And Learning

Every child learns differently, but this is especially the case for children with autism. Some may excel in certain subjects, but struggle in others. Some may need extra support with communication or focus. However, with the right understanding and tools, autistic children can thrive in school and beyond.

This chapter offers practical tips for supporting learning at home, in the classroom, as well as everywhere in between.

1. Understand The Individual

No two autistic learners will ever be the same.

Some may:

- Be highly verbal and love to read
- Struggle with speech and prefer non-verbal communication
- Learn best through pictures, repetition or hands-on activities

Take time to learn how they learn.

Ask:

- What helps them focus?
- What distracts or overwhelms them?
- What subjects excite them?

When you build on their strengths, learning becomes more effective and more joyful.

2. Use Visual Supports

Visual tools can help make learning more understandable and less stressful.

Try using:

- **Picture schedules** for daily routines
- **Step-by-step charts** for tasks, such as brushing teeth or doing homework
- **Visual timers** to show how much time is left
- **Social stories** to explain new situations or rules

Visuals give information in a way that many autistic learners find easier to understand and remember.

3. Build A Predictable Environment

Learning happens best in a calm and structured setting.

You can help by:

- Keeping routines consistent
- Having clear classroom rules or expectations
- Letting them know ahead of time about changes, such as a supply teacher or a school trip

Predictability reduces anxiety and helps students stay focused.

4. Use Flexible Teaching Methods

Autistic students may need lessons adapted to fit their needs. This is called **differentiated instruction**.

Some Ideas:

- Use **hands-on materials** for maths and science
- Allow **extra time** on assignments or tests
- Provide **breaks** during long tasks

Flexibility does not mean lowering expectations, but it means removing unnecessary barriers.

5. Support Communication And Interaction

Whether a student uses words, sign language, pictures or a communication device, the goal is the same! Help them to express themselves and connect with others.

Encourage:

- Peer or small group work
- Turn-taking games or role-playing conversations
- Communication apps or AAC (Augmentative and Alternative Communication) when required

Make space for different communication styles and celebrate every success.

6. EHCP

Children with autism can have an **EHCP** (Education, Health, Care Plan) to help them at school.

These plans might include:

- **One-to-one support**
- **Sensory breaks**
- **Special seating**
- **Help with transitions or social skills**

This is usually reviewed annually to track how they are getting on and whether they have met their targets.

7. Celebrate Progress, Not Just Perfection

Some days will be smooth and others will be tough. But every step forward, no matter how small, is worth celebrating.

Did they stay in class all day? Did they try something new? Did they make a new friend? That is progress!

Keep the focus on growth and not comparison. Every child makes progress at their own pace, which is totally normal.

Final Thought

Autistic learners have so much to offer. With understanding, patience and the right tools, they can shine in school and go far beyond. The most important thing a teacher or parent can do is believe in their potential, even when the path looks different!

Chapter 6: Autism In Teenagers And Adults

Autism does not end in childhood. In fact, many people are not diagnosed until they are teenagers or adults. Whether diagnosed early or later on in life, autistic individuals continue to grow, learn and face new challenges and opportunities through every stage of life.

This chapter explores what autism can look like during the teenage and adult years and how to offer support through big transitions and everyday experiences.

1. The Teenage Years: Change And Growth

The teenage years are a time of major change for everyone. However, for autistic teenagers, the shift can feel even more intense.

They may face:

- **Increased social pressure** (fitting in, making friends or understanding peer dynamics)
- **Body and hormonal changes**
- **New academic demands** and life skills that are challenging
- **Emotional ups and downs** that are hard to name or manage

Tip: Be patient. Offer extra guidance in areas like hygiene, emotional expression and understanding relationships. Don't assume they should know just because they have reached a certain age.

2. Supporting Independence

Teenagers and adults with autism often want more independence, but may need some guidance learning the steps to get there.

Support them in:

- **Daily living skills** (such as, cooking, cleaning, shopping and using public transportation)

- **Time management and organisation**

- **Problem-solving and making choices**

Break tasks into small steps. Use reminders, checklists and routines. It is also very important to always allow space for them to make mistakes and learn from them.

3. Social Life And Friendships

Autistic teenagers and adults may want friendships and relationships, but may struggle with unspoken social rules.

Help by:

- Talking openly about how friendships work (for example, how to start a conversation, respect boundaries or deal with conflict)
- Connecting them with **clubs** or **online communities** related to their interests
- Encouraging social time that respects their comfort zone (such as, small groups, quiet settings or shared activities)

Some may also identify as **neurodivergent** and feel more at ease with others who understand their communication style.

4. Education And Employment

Some autistic people attend college or university. Others pursue vocational training, apprenticeships or enter the workforce directly.

To support their success:

- Look into **Special Educational Needs (SEN) services** at schools or universities
- Explore **job coaching**, **internships** and **supported employment schemes**
- Focus on **strengths and passions** when choosing career paths

Workplaces that value neurodiversity are becoming more common, which is good for everyone.

5. Mental Health Matters

Teenagers and adults with autism may experience:

- **Anxiety**
- **Depression**
- **Burnout** from trying to mask their differences

It is important to find professionals who understand autism. Therapy, peer support or simply having safe spaces to be themselves can make a huge difference.

Note: Masking is when autistic people hide their natural behaviours to fit in. While it can help them navigate certain situations, it can also be exhausting and harmful to their mental health over time.

6. Self-Advocacy And Identity

Many autistic adults are proud of who they are and want to be heard, not fixed. They may speak up about inclusion, accessibility and their rights.

Support self-advocacy by:

- Encouraging decision-making
- Respecting communication preferences

- Listening to their voice and honouring their experiences

Autistic adults are the best experts on autism. When in doubt, ask and learn from them directly.

Final Thought

Autism is a lifelong journey, not a childhood phase. With the right support, teenagers and adults on the spectrum can lead full, independent and meaningful lives. They can build relationships, contribute to their communities and define success on their own terms.

The key is respect, patience and believing in their potential every step of the way!

Chapter 7: Talking About Autism

Talking openly and respectfully about autism is one of the most important things we can do to create understanding. Whether you are a parent, teacher, friend or autistic yourself, how we speak about autism can shape how others think and feel about it, especially children.

This chapter offers guidance on how to have kind, honest and age-appropriate conversations about autism with children, adults and the wider community.

1. Why It Is Important To Talk About Autism

Autism is nothing to be ashamed of. It is simply a different way of thinking, feeling and experiencing the world. When we talk about autism:

- We **reduce stigma**
- We **build empathy**
- We **empower** autistic people to understand and accept themselves
- We help others know how to be more inclusive and supportive

Silence can create confusion or shame. Open conversations create clarity and connection.

2. How To Talk To A Child About Their Autism

If your child is autistic, it is important to talk to them about it in a positive, honest and age-appropriate way. You do not have to have all the answers, but you just need to start the conversation!

You might say:

- 'Everyone's brain works in its own way. Your brain works differently and that is called autism.'

- 'You might notice things other people don't or get upset when things change. That is part of autism and it is totally fine.'

- 'Autism is part of who you are. It does not mean something is wrong with you! It just means you see the world differently.'

Use books, cartoons or stories to help explain. Let them ask questions and remind them they are loved just the way they are.

3. How To Talk To Others About Autism

Sometimes, you will need to talk to others, such as family, teachers or classmates about autism.

Tips for respectful conversations:

- **Start with strengths**: 'He is really creative and has a great memory for facts.'

- **Explain differences calmly**: 'She might not look at you when you talk, but she is still listening.'

- **Correct misunderstandings gently**: 'Autism is not caused by bad parenting. It is just how the brain is wired.'

- **Speak up when needed** especially if someone uses hurtful or outdated language.

4. Encouraging Inclusion And Understanding

Teach children and adults that differences are normal and valuable. Encourage kindness, curiosity and compassion.

You might say:

- 'Some people talk with their hands, some use words and some use pictures. All of those are absolutely fine!'

- 'It is okay if someone plays differently or does not like loud sounds. We all like different things.'

Promote inclusive books, movies and classroom activities. The more people see autism in everyday life, the more normal and accepted it becomes.

5. Dealing With Myths And Misunderstandings

Sadly, some people still believe myths, such as 'autistic people do not have feelings' or 'all autistic people are the same.' These ideas are wrong and harmful.

You can gently share the truth:

- Autistic people feel deeply, even if they express it differently.
- Autism is a spectrum. No two autistic people are the same.
- Many autistic people lead rich, full lives with careers and relationships.

Remember: education and empathy go hand in hand.

Final Thought

Talking about autism is a powerful way to create change. When we speak honestly and kindly, we help build a world where autistic people are understood, included and respected. They should not just be tolerated, but truly welcomed in every setting.

So, talk openly, listen deeply and keep the conversation going.

Chapter 8: Myths And Truths About Autism

There are many myths and misunderstandings about autism. These myths can cause confusion, fear or unfair treatment. In this chapter, we will set the record straight by breaking down some of the most common myths and sharing the real truth behind them.

Understanding the facts helps everyone support and respect autistic people fully.

Myth 1: 'Autism is caused by bad parenting.'

→ Truth: Autism is not caused by parenting style.

Autism is a neurodevelopmental difference, which means it is how a person's brain develops. It is not caused by being 'too strict' or 'too soft' as a parent. There is no single known cause of autism, but research shows it involves a mix of genetics and biology, not parenting.

Myth 2: 'Autistic people don't have feelings.'

→ Truth: Autistic people feel deeply, just like anyone else.

Autistic people may express their emotions differently, but that does not mean they do not feel love, joy, sadness or empathy. In fact, many autistic people are very sensitive and caring. It may just look different from what others expect.

Myth 3: 'All autistic people are the same.'

→ Truth: Autism is a spectrum and every autistic person is unique.

Some autistic people need a lot of support, while others live independently. Some talk a lot, while others do not speak at all. Some love routine, while others enjoy trying out new things. There is no one 'autistic way' to be, just like there is no one 'typical' way to be human.

Myth 4: 'Autistic people don't want friends.'

→ Truth: Many autistic people want connection, but socialising can be hard.

Autistic people may struggle with social rules or communication, but that does not mean they do not want friends. They might just prefer smaller groups, different kinds of interaction or need more time to build trust. Relationships matter to them, but in their own way.

Myth 5: 'Autism is a disease that needs to be cured.'

→ Truth: Autism is not a disease; it is a different way of being.

Autism is not something to 'fix.' It is not an illness. It is a part of who someone is. While support and therapy can help with certain challenges, the goal is not to change who the person is. The goal is to help them thrive as they are.

Myth 6: 'Autistic people are not smart.'

→ Truth: Intelligence and autism are not the same thing.

Some autistic people have intellectual disabilities, but many have average or above-average intelligence. Some are gifted in certain areas, such as music, memory or maths. Intelligence shows up in many ways, not just in school grades or IQ tests.

Myth 7: 'You can tell someone is autistic just by looking at them.'

→ Truth: You cannot always 'see' autism.

Autism is not always visible. Some people 'mask' their symptoms to fit in, while others may not have obvious behaviours. That does not make their experiences any less real. Always believe someone when they tell you they are autistic, even if it does not match what you expected.

Myth 8: 'Only boys are autistic.'

→ Truth: Autism affects both genders.

Boys are diagnosed more often, but girls can be autistic too. Sometimes, they are missed or diagnosed incorrectly because they present differently or are better at masking. It is important to recognise that boys are not the only ones that are autistic.

Final Thought

When we replace myths with facts, we make the world a better place for autistic people and for everyone around us. The more we learn, the more we grow in kindness, understanding and inclusion.

Always ask questions, stay open-minded and be willing to challenge stereotypes. The truth is that autism is not a problem to be solved, but a difference to be respected.

Chapter 9: How To Be A Good Ally

Being an ally means standing beside someone, supporting them and helping others understand and include them too. When it comes to autism, allies play an important role. Whether you are a parent, friend, teacher, classmate, co-worker or just someone that cares, you can help create a kinder and more accepting world.

This chapter offers simple and meaningful ways to be a good ally to autistic people of all ages.

1. Listen To Autistic Voices

One of the best ways to understand autism is to learn from autistic people themselves. They are the true experts of their own experiences.

- Follow autistic advocates online
- Read books or watch videos by autistic creators
- Ask respectful questions and listen to the answers

Tip: Instead of speaking for autistic people, help make space for them to speak for themselves.

2. Respect Differences

Autistic people may act, speak or move differently, which is totally fine.

They might:

- Avoid eye contact
- Use a device to talk
- Flap their hands or rock when excited or nervous
- Speak very directly or focus deeply on a special interest

These behaviours are not 'wrong.' They are just different ways and that is okay. Respecting those differences is a big part of being a good ally.

3. Use Kind And Inclusive Language

The words we use matter. Avoid saying things like 'we all have a little autism' or calling autism a 'tragedy.' These comments may seem small, but they can hurt.

Use terms that autistic people prefer and always speak with kindness and accuracy. If you are not sure what language to use, just ask!

4. Stand Up Against Bullying Or Exclusion

If you see someone being left out, teased or judged for being different, say or do something.

- Invite them to join in
- Say, 'that is not okay' if someone makes fun of them
- Talk to a teacher, adult or manager if needed

Even quiet actions, such as sitting with someone who is alone, can make a big difference.

5. Make Room For Everyone

In classrooms, workplaces and social spaces, look for ways to make things more accessible and welcoming.

You can help by:

- Encouraging group activities that include different types of learners
- Asking what support someone needs
- Avoiding loud and chaotic environments when possible
- Celebrating strengths and wins in many forms, rather than just relying on test scores or popularity

Inclusion is not about 'letting' someone be part of something. It is about building things that work for everyone from the start.

6. Be Patient And Open-Minded

Sometimes, communication may take longer. Sometimes, someone might say something unexpected. Don't rush, interrupt or assume you know best.

Instead:

- Wait and give time to respond
- Ask clear and direct questions

- Offer support rather than correction

Remember, patience shows respect.

7. Support Fairness, Not Sameness

Being fair does not mean treating everyone exactly the same. It means giving people what they need to succeed.

If someone gets extra time on a test, a fidget toy or a quiet break, it is not 'special treatment.' It is just what helps them learn or feel safe.

8. Keep Learning

No one knows everything, but everyone can keep learning.

Being a good ally means being willing to:

- Admit when you don't know something
- Listen when someone shares their story

Remember, growth is part of allyship.

Final Thought

You don't need to be perfect to be a great ally. You just need to be kind, curious, respectful and willing to listen. Your support, your voice and your example can help build a world where autistic people are accepted, supported and celebrated, just as they are.

Being an ally is not a one-time act. It is a lifelong commitment to fairness, compassion and community.

Chapter 10: Resources And Next Steps

You have made it to the final chapter, so well done! Whether you are a parent, teacher, sibling, friend or someone who is autistic yourself, I hope this guide has helped you understand autism a little better and feel more confident in supporting and celebrating neurodiversity.

In this chapter, we will explore next practical steps and useful resources to keep learning, connecting and growing.

1. Keep Learning

Autism is a broad and complex topic, so the learning never really ends. Keep reading, listening and exploring.

Here are a few ways to continue:

- **Books**: Look for books written by autistic people. Their perspectives are invaluable.

- **Podcasts And Videos**: Many autistic advocates share their stories and tips online.

- **Websites**: Trusted organisations usually offer free articles, toolkits and training.

Tip: Be cautious of resources that talk about 'curing' autism or only focus on the challenges. Look for materials that value acceptance, not just awareness.

2. Connect With Community

You are not alone. Whether you are autistic or supporting someone who is, connection makes a difference.

Ways to connect:

- **Online communities and forums**
- **Local support groups** for parents, families or autistic adults
- **Social groups** based on shared interests (like gaming, music or books)

Connection reduces isolation and offers support, advice and encouragement.

3. Support Autistic Voices

Amplify autistic voices in your community and beyond.

- Share their books, blogs and videos.
- Invite autistic speakers to schools or workplaces.
- Donate to organisations led by autistic people.

Nothing about autism should be decided without autistic input.

4. Take Action In Your Everyday Life

Small actions everyday can lead to big changes.

- Speak up when you hear stereotypes.

- Make classrooms, homes and workplaces more inclusive.

- Practice patience and curiosity with others.

- Encourage children to be kind, ask questions and celebrate differences.

Change does not always come from big events. It often starts with quiet and consistent kindness.

5. Helpful Organisations And Websites

(Note: Depending on your country, local resources may vary. Here are some widely respected global resources to begin with.)

- **Autistic Self Advocacy Network (ASAN)** – autisticadvocacy.org
  Advocacy and resources by and for autistic people.

- **Autism Speaks** – autismspeaks.org
  Offers a variety of toolkits and information.

- **National Autistic Society (UK)** – autism.org.uk
  Great resources for education, work and support in the UK.

- **NeuroClastic** – neuroclastic.com
  Articles and insights written by neurodivergent individuals.

- **The Autism Helper** – theautismhelper.com
  Practical resources for teachers and caregivers.

6. A Final Word Of Encouragement

Autism is not something to be feared or fixed, it is something to be understood and embraced.

Autistic people are artists, scientists, parents, teachers, thinkers and dreamers. They bring unique strengths, insights and beauty to our world.

If you remember just one thing from this book, let it be this:

Autistic people don't need to be changed to fit the world. The world needs to grow to include everyone.

And that change starts with learning, listening and loving people just the way they are.

You Are Not Done, You Are Just Beginning

Thank you for reading this guide. I hope it gave you clarity, comfort and a sense of direction. Now that you know more, go out and be the kind of person, parent, friend or teacher who makes the world safer and more inclusive for autistic people everywhere.

Remember, understanding autism does not end with a book, it begins with your everyday choices!